S0-CWU-830

# The Renaissance

by Claire Barberini

PEARSON

Glenview, Illinois • Boston, Massachusetts • Chandler, Arizona
Upper Saddle River, New Jersey

artist

ceiling

Michelangelo was an artist. He made beautiful paintings. This painting was on the ceiling of a church.

Long ago, a special time began in Europe. It was called the Renaissance. People had new ideas. They made new things. They made beautiful art.

The Renaissance began in Italy in the 1300s. It lasted about 300 years.

Renaissance is a French word. It means "a time when things are discovered again." Discover means "to find."

During the Renaissance, people found books that were lost for a long time. They found lost art. People talked about these ideas again.

## Extend Language    Prefix *re-*

Prefixes are added to the front of words. They change what the words mean. What does the prefix *re-* mean?

- *redo* means "do again"
- *rewrite* means "write again"
- *rediscover* means "discover again"

The Renaissance moved to other countries.

In Poland, there was an astronomer named Copernicus. An astronomer studies space. Copernicus discovered new things about the sun and the planets.

sun

In France, there was a man named Descartes. He was a great thinker. He wrote new ideas about right and wrong.

Descartes

ships

In Spain, the king and queen sent Christopher Columbus across the ocean. He sailed on ships to find new lands. He found the Americas.

In Italy, Leonardo da Vinci had a new idea for a flying machine. He never built it. His ideas are still famous today.

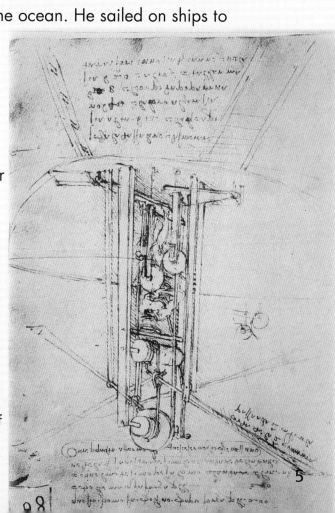

Da Vinci's drawing of his flying machine

People used ideas from long ago to make new art.

In England, Shakespeare wrote plays. Many people went to see his plays.

Raphael was an artist in Italy. He painted beautiful pictures for churches.

picture

a play

## Extend Language    Action Verbs

Action verbs tell of doing something. For example, "I *eat* an apple." *Eat* is the action verb.

Here are some examples from this book.

| Example Sentence | | Action Verb |
|---|---|---|
| • They found lost art. | ⟶ | found |
| • They made new things. | ⟶ | made |
| • The Renaissance began in Italy. | ⟶ | began |

Can you find two action verbs on this page?

Today, many people still enjoy watching plays.

Like Michelangelo, artists today paint pictures on buildings.

People today still use Renaissance ideas. We have great writers and artists. People make new things. Thinkers have new ideas.

What new ideas will you have?